T0001932

sealf-care
for everyone

sealf-care
for everyone

Wang XX

THE EXPERIMENT

NEW YORK

Sealf-Care for Everyone
Text and illustrations copyright © 2023 by Fanqiao Wang

Originally published in Great Britain by Orion Spring, an imprint of The Orion
Publishing Group Limited, in 2023. First published in North America in revised form
by The Experiment, LLC, in 2024.

The Experiment, LLC
220 East 23rd Street, Suite 600
New York, NY 10010-4658
theexperimentpublishing.com

THE EXPERIMENT and its colophon are registered trademarks of
The Experiment, LLC.

The Experiment's books are available at special discounts when purchased in bulk
for premiums and sales promotions as well as for fund-raising or educational use.
For details, contact us at info@theexperimentpublishing.com.

Library of Congress Cataloging-in-Publication Data available upon request

ISBN 978-1-61519-986-0
Ebook ISBN 978-1-61519-988-4

Cover illustration by Wang XX

Manufactured in China

First printing March 2024
10 9 8 7 6 5 4 3 2 1

meet yoursealf

---

love yoursealf

---

be kind to yoursealf

---

embrace yoursealf

meet yoursealf

I don't wanna go to work.
I don't wanna go to bed.

I don't wanna go out.
I don't wanna go home.

I'm trying to push my limits!

Thinking gives me a headache

and headache makes me think.

I'm actually
incredibly blue
but you
will never
know.

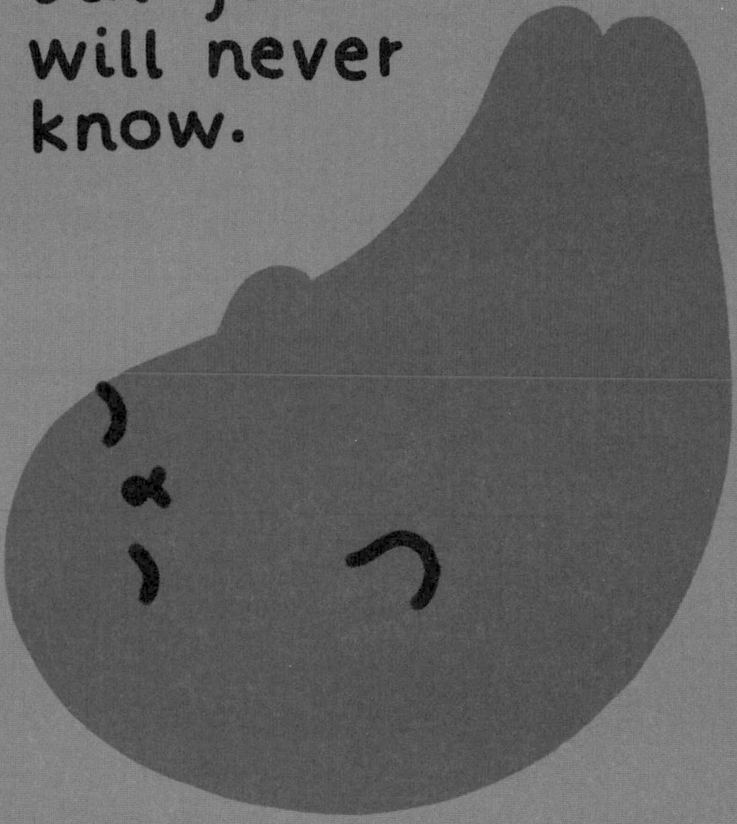

I'm pretty uncomfortable right now,
and I'm not pretending I'm fine.

WHO AM I ?
Where did I
come from?

WHERE should
I go?

I feel a bit complicated at the moment but I think I'm able to deal with it.

TODAY

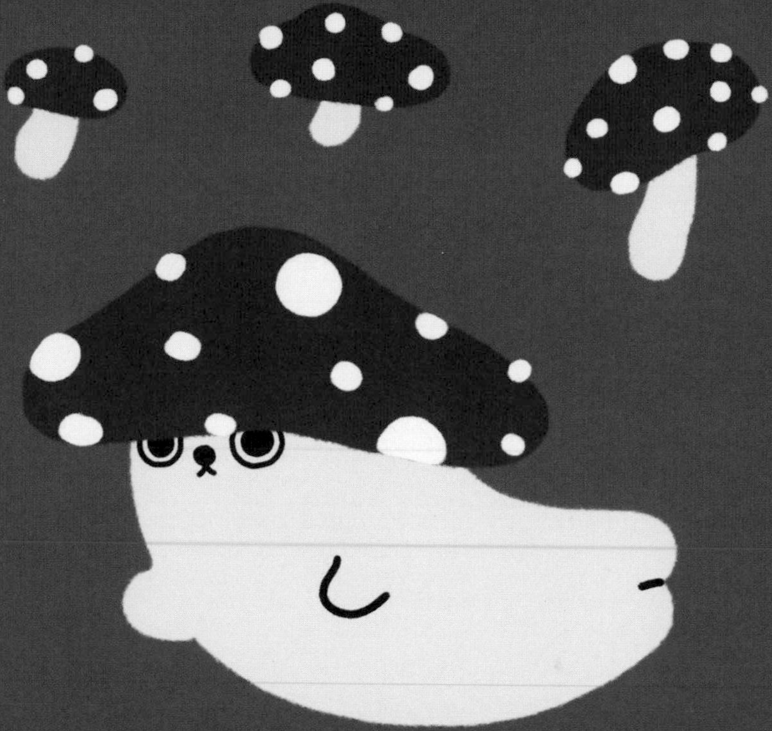

I'm a mushroom and I don't feel like talking to anyone.

I'm full of questions,

and I've decided to
ignore all of them.

I wanna live a simple life,
and feel rich feelings.

I just forgot what I-m supposed to do

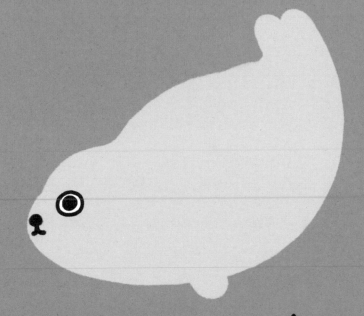

and I think it's Ok.

I'm too small to change anything

but I'm too
adorable to
be ignored.

When I'm not under any pressure,

I feel a sweet emptiness.

I think ......

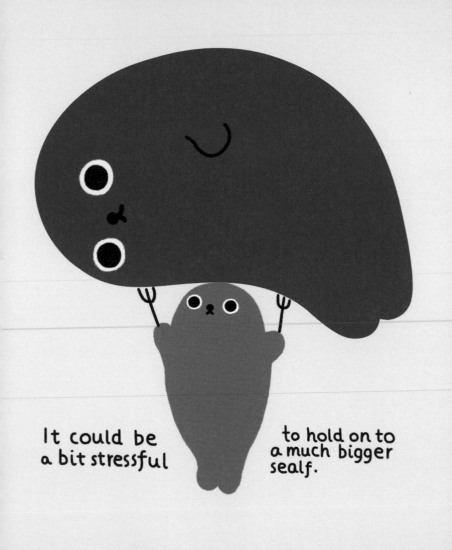

It could be
a bit stressful

to hold on to
a much bigger
sealf.

I'm incredibly sealy.

love yoursealf

I deserve more, don't I ?

Yes, you
do!

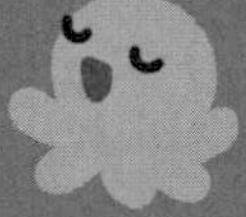

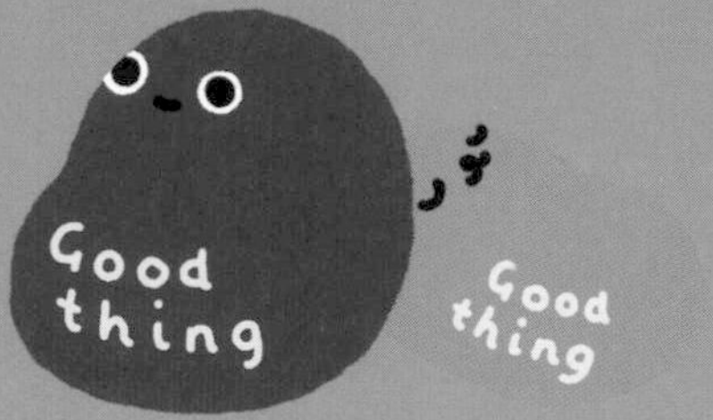
Good thing
Good thing

I deserve all the good things!

Even though I don't have them yet.

I deserve a better world

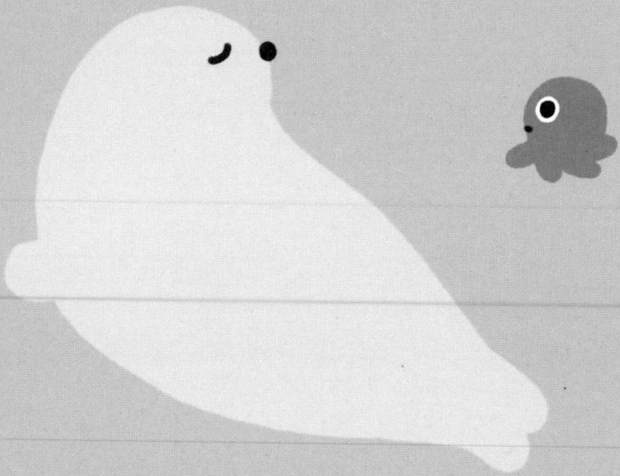

and so do you

You know what ?

No one can force me to do anything.

I'm so small.

But that's not a problem at all!

I don't care if you're rich or powerful.

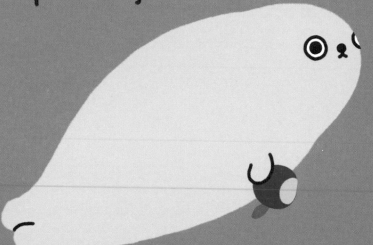

I do care if you love your-sealf and feel relaxed.

I care.

I will not leave you empty.

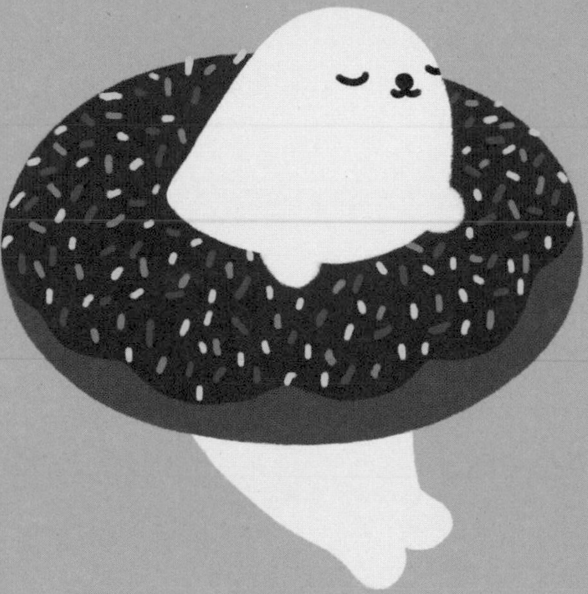

I can't sleep
tonight.

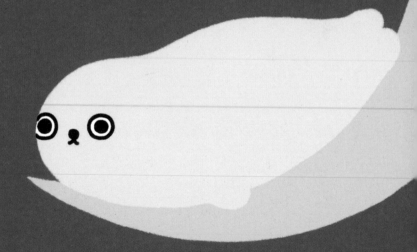

and it's ok.

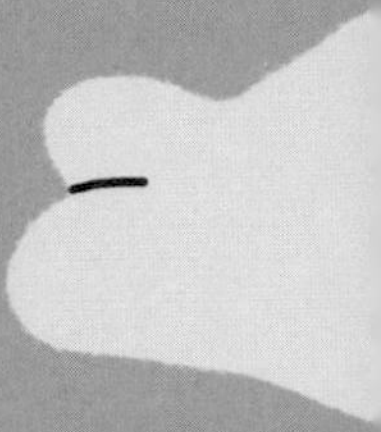

I'm not getting close
to that fluffy mat.

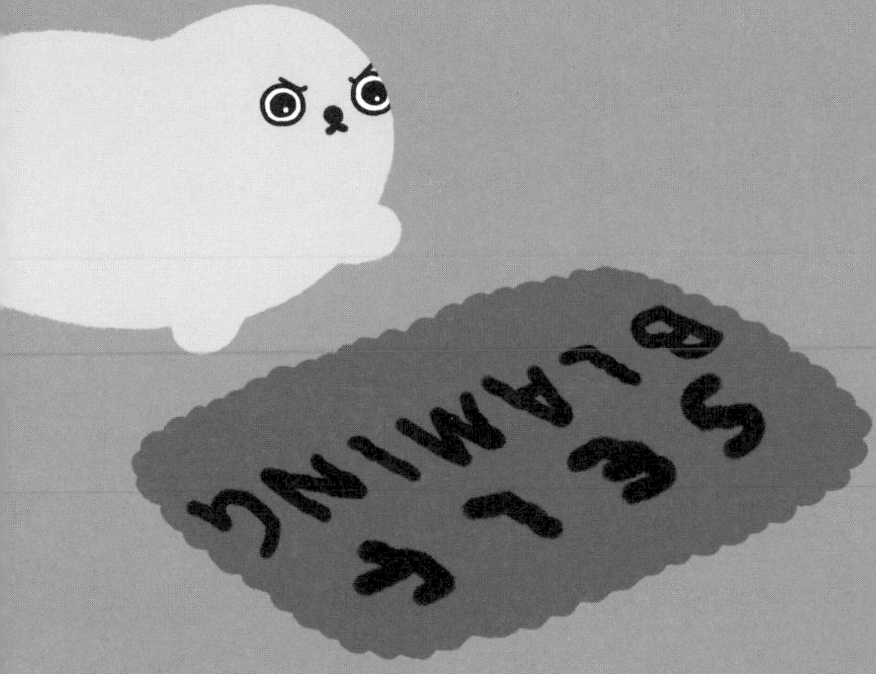
SELF
BLAMING

Maybe I should forget everything that bothered me ......

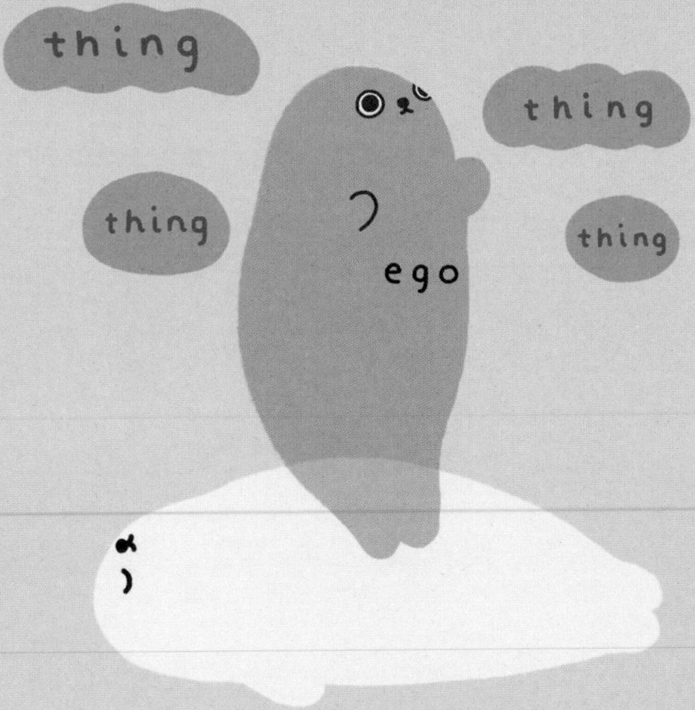
thing
thing
thing
thing
ego

and the ego that made me feel bothered.

I don't need to change mysealf for anybody.

I change because I feel like it.

Please don't wake me up ……

until I'm bored of sleeping.

be kind to yoursealf

Don't ever try to hide
your heart.

Here is the only thing I have and I'm gonna give it to you.

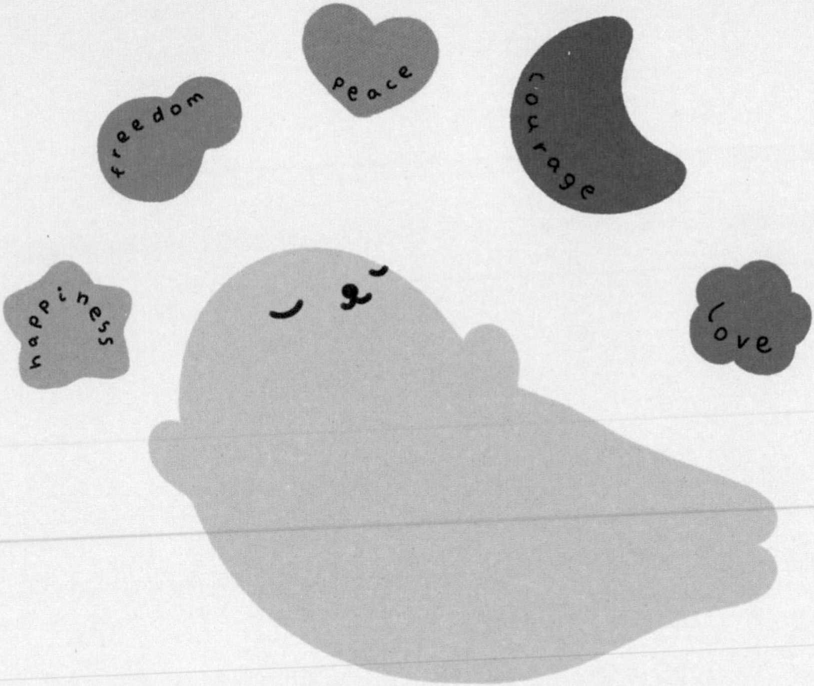
freedom
peace
courage
happiness
love

You deserve all of this!

Just relax and let your body flow.

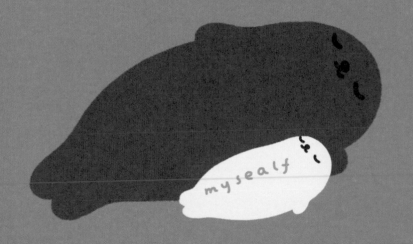

Hold yoursealf if you can.

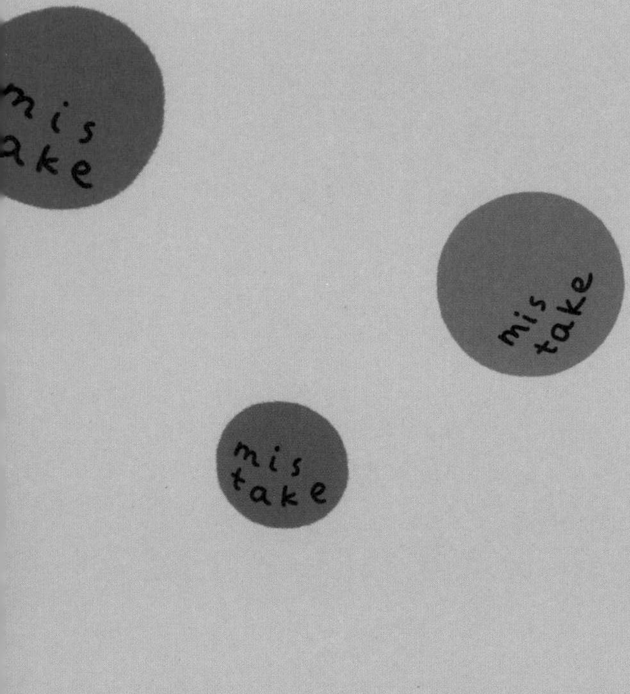

mistake

mistake

mistake

It's ok to make mistakes, my friend.

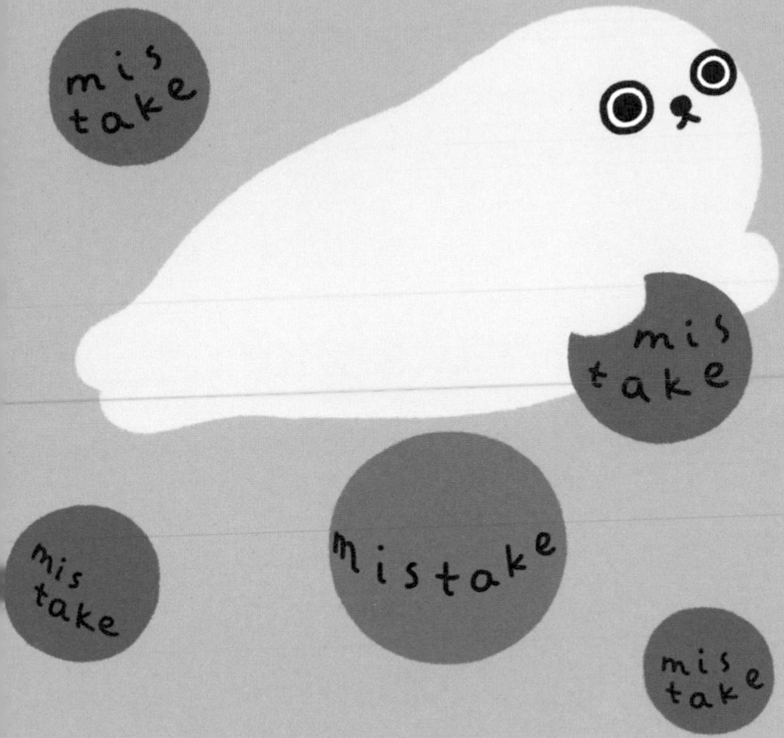
mis take
mis take
mis take
mistake
mis take

It's ok!

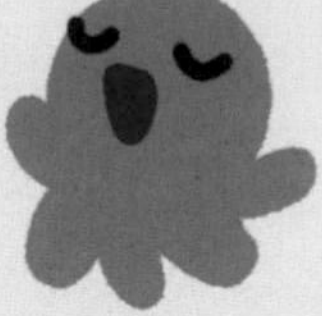

There are too many
things that you can't
control and I can't
either.

You can do better,

but you don't have
to.

No you can't
blame seal

or little octopus
Or yoursealf

goal
goal
goal
goal
goal

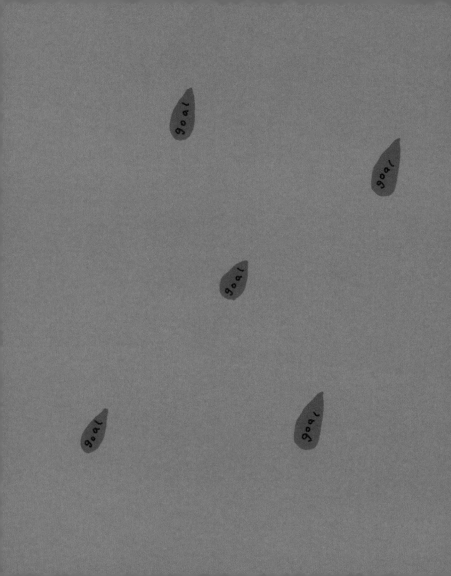

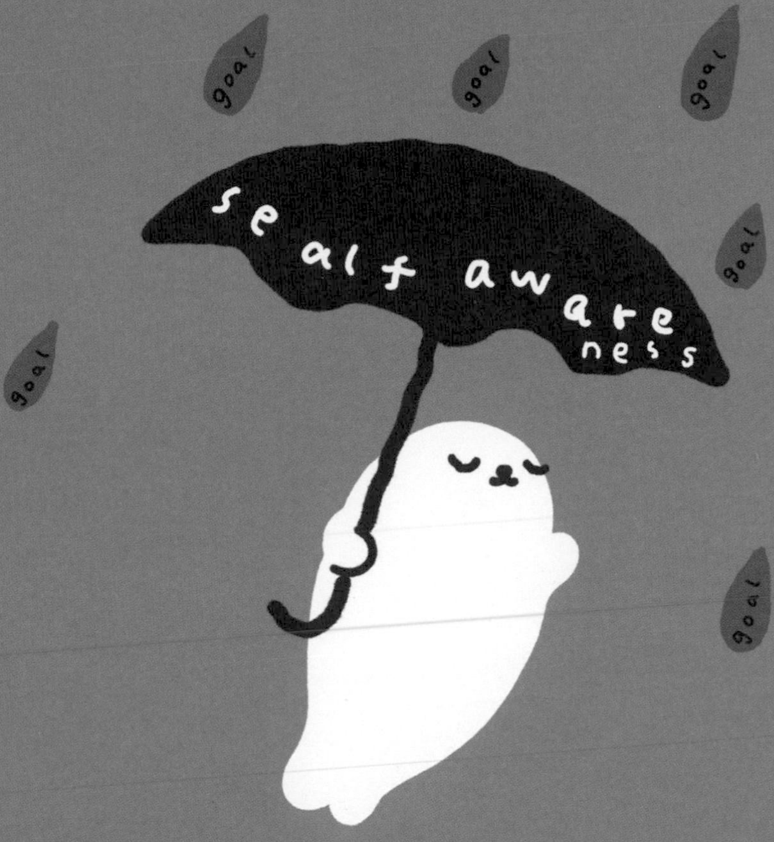
goal
goal
goal
goal
goal
goal
sealf awareness

You don't need to meet any goals that you don't really care about deeply in your soul.

You've already tried your best,

and whatever you're
going through is not
your fault.

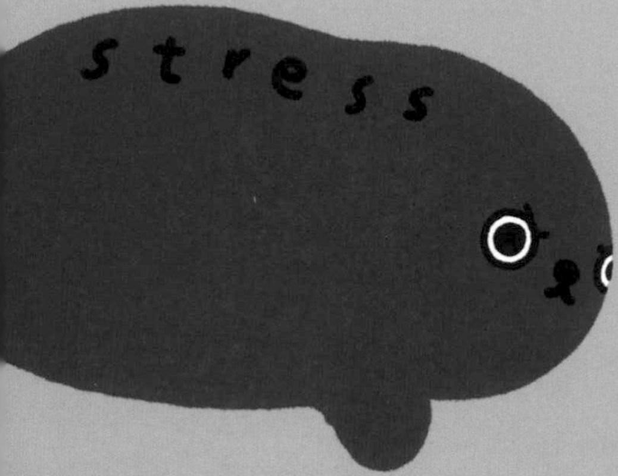
stress

When stress comes, let it lie down by your side.

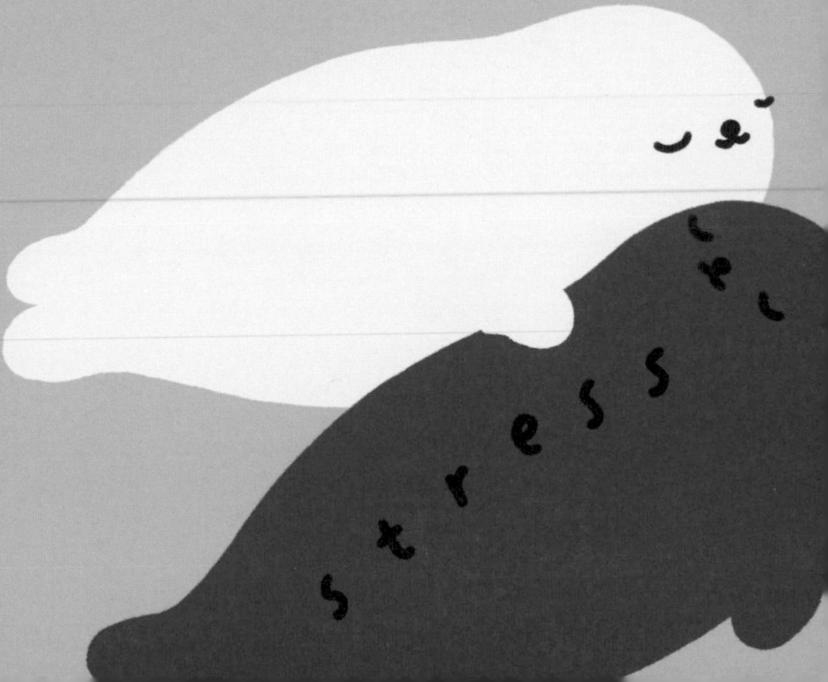
stress

Time to stretch!

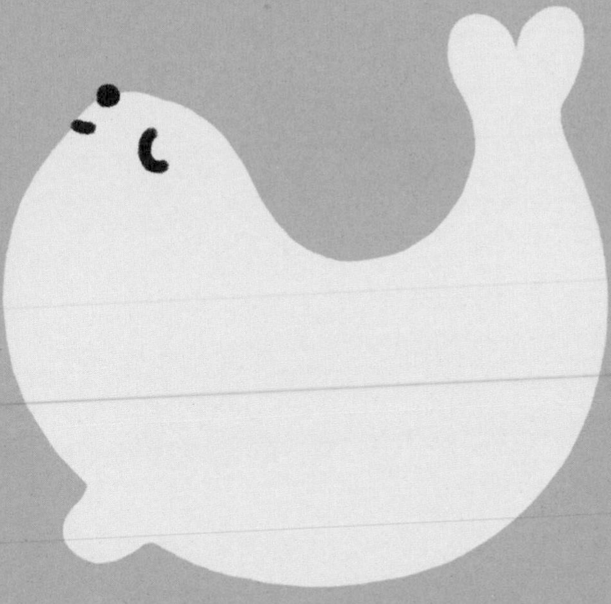

Leave your desk!

Come on, give
me a hug.

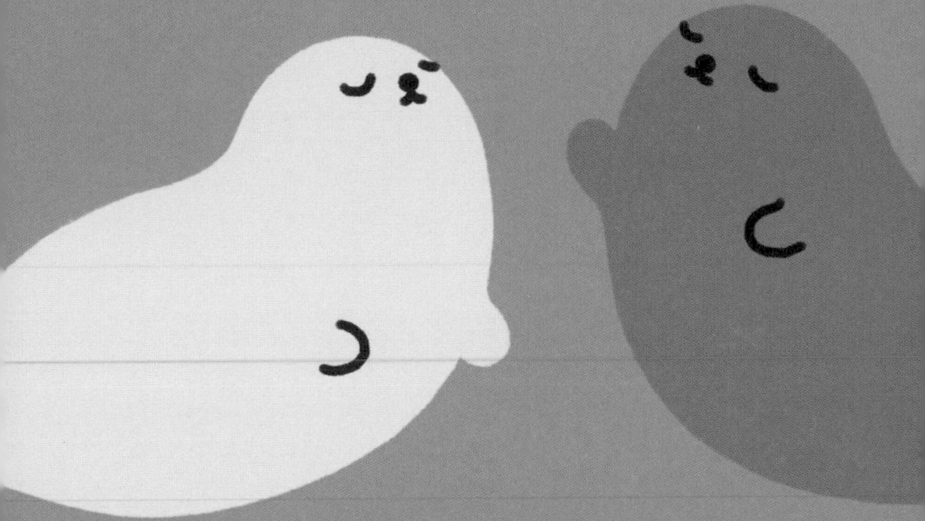

I know you
need one.

embrace yoursealf

Come here, baby,

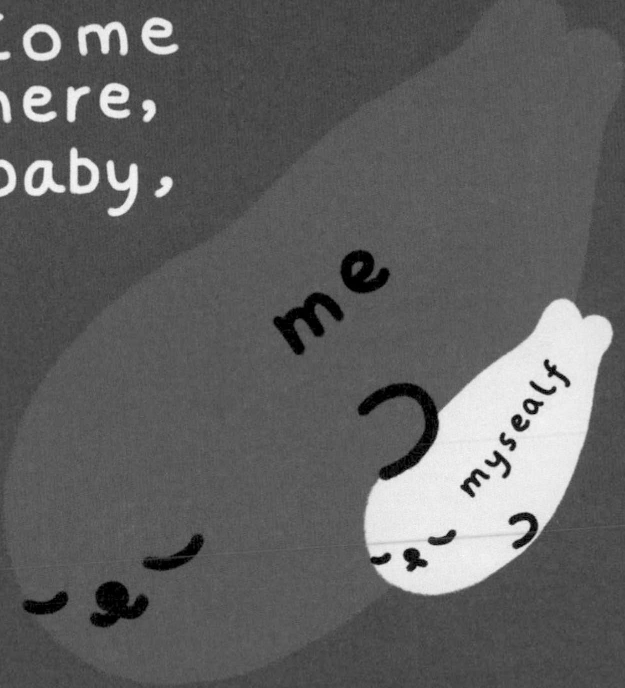

I'll take care of you.

Please come to my palm
when you feel blue.

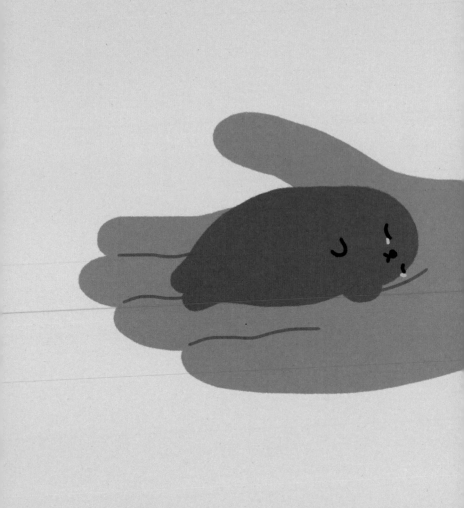

unknown
noises

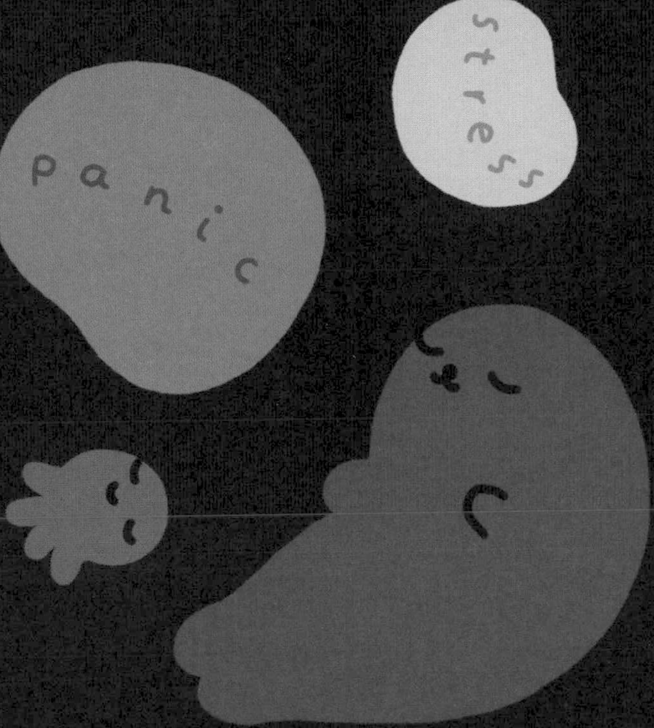
panic
stress

Time to let go!

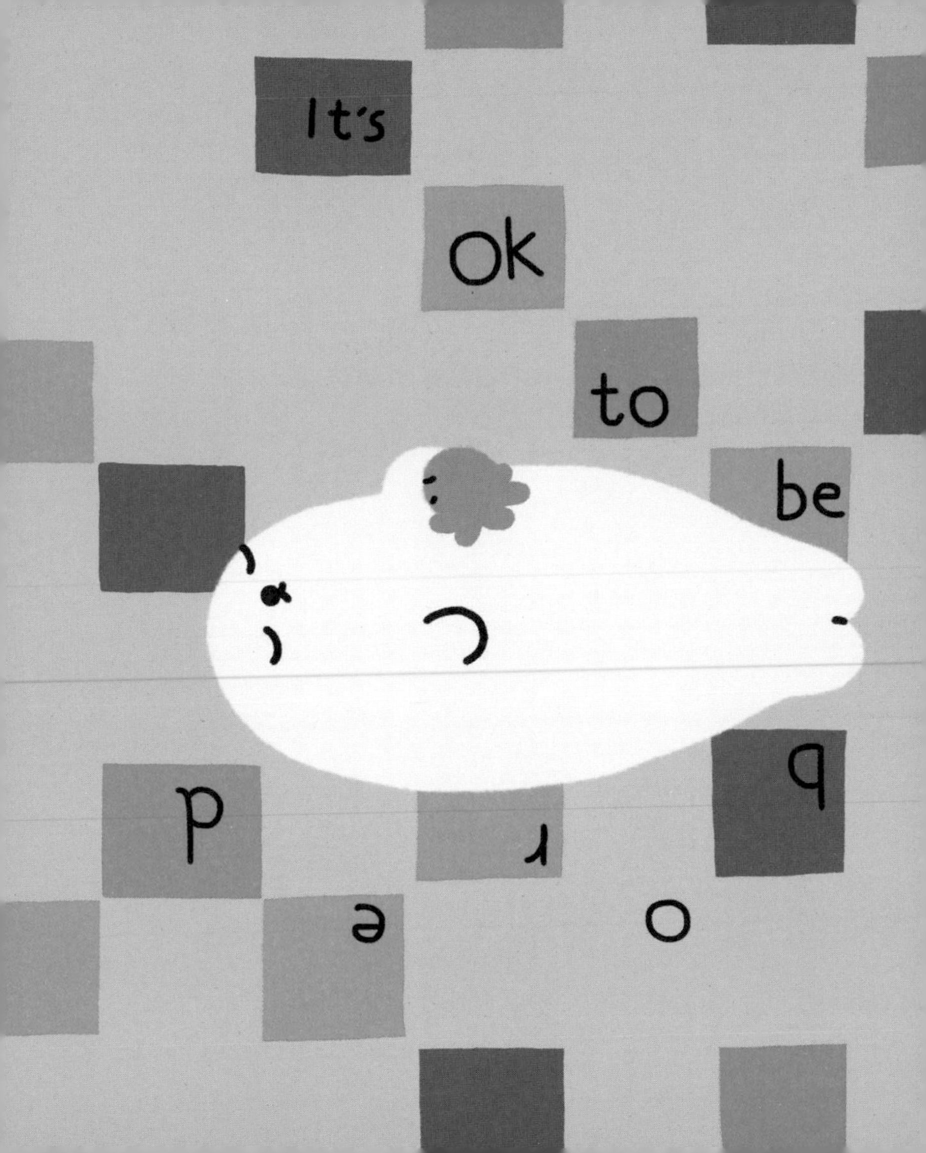
It's
OK
to
be
bored

No need to make any effort,
you are special already.

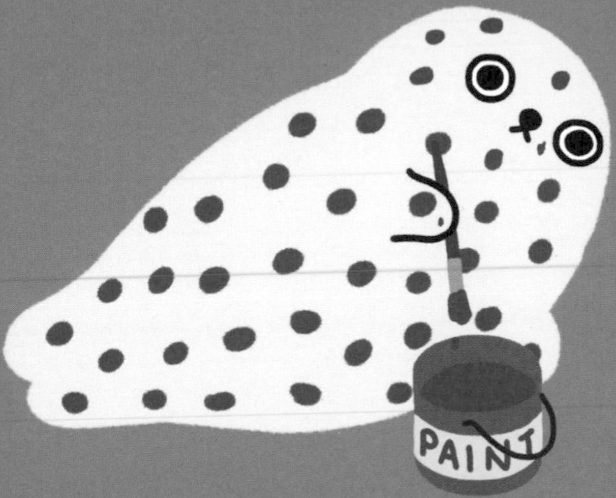
PAINT

All we need is to rest.

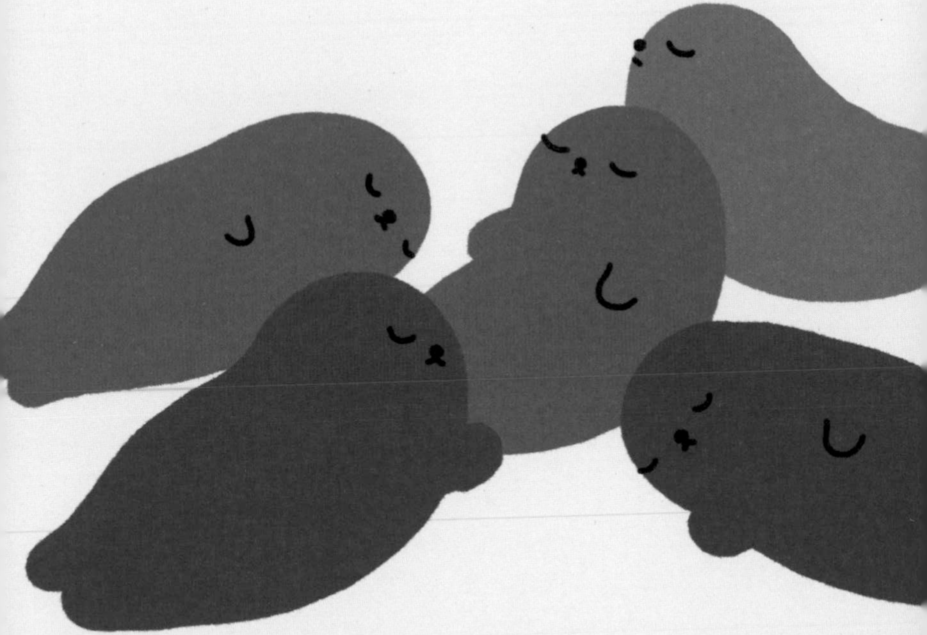

Something annoys me and I'm
resting on it.

I'm resting underneath my own anger.

I'm resting on the dark side of me.

I accept each and every side of me as who I am.

I'm relying on mysealf

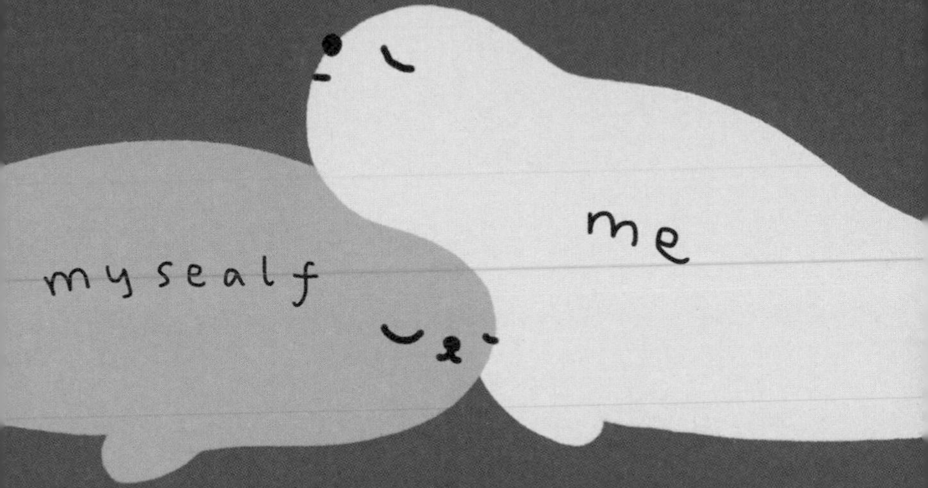
me
mysealf

100% and feel very secure about it.

I'm not thinking about anything right now and it feels just beautiful.

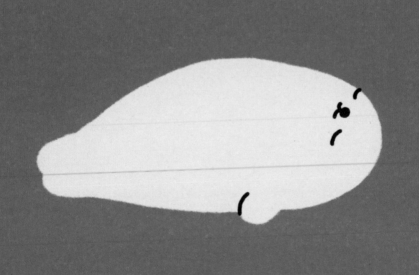

Come with me,

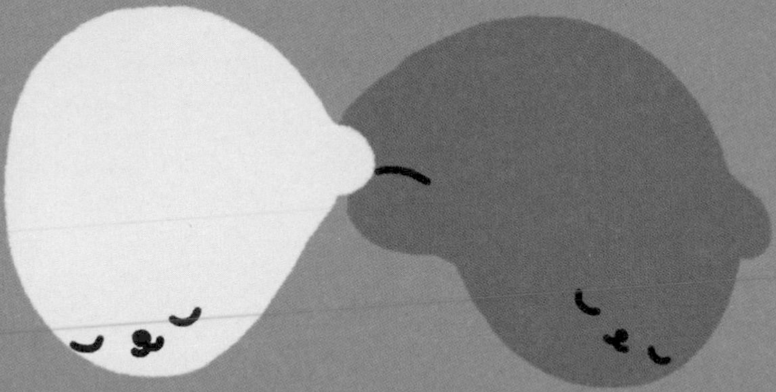

and let's do nothing together!

Little octopus
will always be
with you.

We are so
ordinary

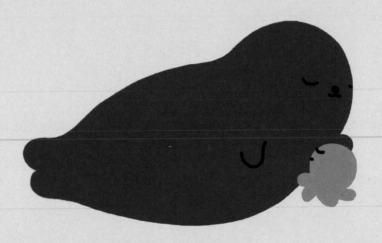

and so precious

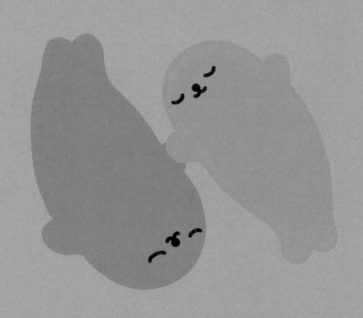

Good night
&
sweet dreams